KU-244-522

# How Animals Grow

Claire Llewellyn

**W**

**FRANKLIN WATTS**

LONDON•SYDNEY

LIBRAH
L
694187      SCH
J591.3

First published in 2005 by Franklin Watts
96 Leonard Street, London EC2A 4XD

Franklin Watts Australia
Level 17/207 Kent Street, Sydney NSW 2000

Text copyright © Claire Llewellyn 2005
Design and concept © Franklin Watts 2005

Series adviser: Gill Matthews, non-fiction literacy
    consultant and Inset trainer
Series editor: Rachel Cooke
Editor: Sarah Ridley
Series design: Peter Scoulding
Designer: Jemima Lumley

Acknowledgements: Henry Ausloos/NHPA 14; Anthony Bannister/NHPA 12; H van den Berg/Still
Pictures imprint page, 21; Frank Blackburn/Ecoscene cover, 10; Laurie Campbell/NHPA 4;
Franklin Watts Library title page; M Harvey/Still Pictures 6;  Daniel Heuclin/NHPA 8, 20; Thomas
D Mangelsen/Still Pictures 15, 23; Luiz C Marigo/Still Pictures 17; Graham Neden/Ecoscene 9,
22r; Fritz Polking/Ecoscene 13; Steve Robinson/NHPA 16; Kevin Schafer/NHPA 11;
Barrie Watts 5, 7, 18, 19, 22l.

All rights reserved. No part of this publication may be reproduced, stored in a retrieval system, or
transmitted in any form or by any means, electronic, mechanical, photocopy, recording or
otherwise, without the prior written permission of the copyright owner.

A CIP catalogue record for this book is available from the British Library.

ISBN: 0 7496 6363 4      ·

Dewey decimal classification number: 571.8'1
Printed in China

# Contents

# Animals and their young

All animals have young. Some baby animals look like their parents. Others don't.

▶ *Lambs look like their mother, only smaller.*

▼ *Baby mice look different from their parents. They have no fur.*

You are an animal, too. What did you look like when you were a baby?

# All alone

Some young animals grow up on their own. Their parents do not look after them.

▶ *Baby turtles hatch and make their own way to the sea.*

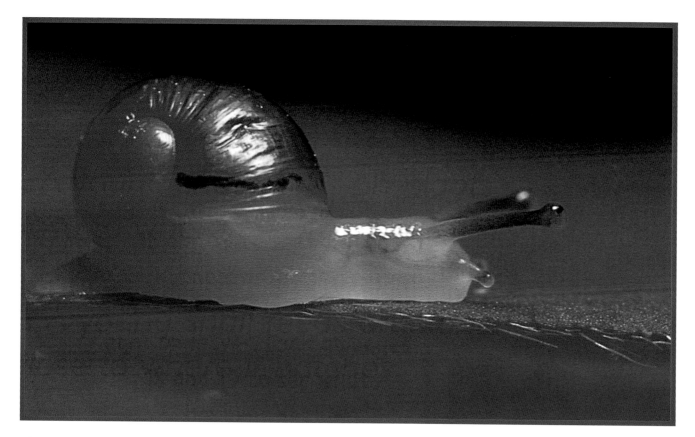

▲ *A young snail feeds on plants close to where it hatches.*

In summer, butterflies lay eggs on leaves. Look at pages 18 and 19 to see what happens next.

# Looking after baby

Some young animals need a lot of care. Their parents look after them.

*◀A scorpion keeps her babies safe by carrying them on her back.*

Who looked after you when you were a baby? How did they look after you?

◀ *Penguin parents take it in turns to keep their chick warm.*

# Feeding and growing

Young animals need food to grow.

▶ *Baby birds feed on insects collected by their parents.*

A zebra feeds on its mother's milk.

# Bigger and stronger

Young animals soon grow bigger and stronger. They begin to run, climb, swim and fly.

►*After a few weeks, a foal can run fast.*

12

When did you first sit up? When did you begin to walk?

◀ *Young lion cubs start to climb trees.*

13

# Learning more

Animals learn many things as they grow older.

▲ *Birds learn to fly.*

Can you think of three things that you have learned to do?

◀ *Young bears learn how to catch fish by watching their parents.*

15

# New kinds of food

As some animals grow bigger, they eat different foods. Many learn to catch it for themselves.

►*This chimp has learned to catch termites with a stick.*

*This fawn still drinks its mother's milk but is starting to eat grass as well.*

What foods do you eat now that you didn't eat when you were a baby?

17

# Changing shape

Some animals grow up in a different way. As they get older, their bodies change shape.

**1** *A caterpillar hatches from an egg and grows bigger as it feeds.*

**2** *After a few weeks, a caterpillar changes into a pupa.*

**3** *Then it changes into a butterfly. It is an adult now.*

Frogs change shape as they grow older. Find out how.

# Fully grown

When an animal is fully grown, it is called an adult. It can have young of its own now.

▲ *Female shrews can have young by the time they are six weeks old.*

▼ *Elephants grow up more slowly. A female has her first calf when she is about 13 years old.*

How old were your parents when they had you?

# I know that...

**1** All animals have young.

**2** Some young animals look after themselves.

**3** Others need a lot of care.

**4** Animals need food to grow.

**5** Growing animals get bigger and stronger.

**6** They learn how to run, climb, swim, fly and hunt.

**7** Some animals eat different kinds of food as they grow up.

**8** Some animals change shape as they get older.

**9** When an animal is fully grown, it is called an adult.

# Index

## About this book

*I Know That!* is designed to introduce children to the process of gathering information and using reference books, one of the key skills needed to begin more formal learning at school. For this reason, each book's structure reflects the information books children will use later in their learning career – with key information in the main text and additional facts and ideas in the captions. The panels give an opportunity for further activities, ideas or discussions. The contents page and index are helpful reference guides.

The language is carefully chosen to be accessible to children just beginning to read. Illustrations support the text but also give information in their own right; active consideration and discussion of images is another key referencing skill. The main aim of the series is to build confidence – showing children how much they already know and giving them the ability to gather new information for themselves. With this in mind, the *I know that...* section at the end of the book is a simple way for children to revisit what they already know as well as what they have learnt from reading the book.